Acknowledgments

Many people have contributed to this book, in a variety of ways.

I would like to thank my parents, Pastor George and Jeanne DeTellis for their steadfast leadership as they serve the poorest of the poor. They are my role models and have laid the foundation for a new generation of leaders in Haiti.

To my writer, Tom Gill, who has well crafted my heart for Haiti and commitment to leadership on the following pages.

To Pat Theriault for his cover design and creative input.

To the team at New Missions, I admire their dedication to the calling. To my assistant, Cheryl Pavuk who took the extra time after hours to read through edits with a passion for the message.

And to my wife, Sheryl, for believing in the power of helping others fulfill their God-given potential.

Finally, to Mike Janiczek with Advantage Books for seeing the potential of this message to impact individuals and then change the lives of future leaders in the third-world.

The best is yet to come.

~ Tim DeTellis

TIMOTHY DeTELLIS

THE
Pearl
OF
LEADERSHIP

SEVEN TREASURES FROM 1804

Advantage™
LEADERSHIP

This book is dedicated to my father, Pastor George DeTellis. I am forever thankful to him because his life is an example of true servant leadership. He gave to people that could never pay him back.

Tim DeTellis

Table of Contents

Introduction 9

Chapter One 11
Welcome to Paradise

Chapter Two 21
Haiti's Fight for Independence

Chapter Three 31
Isolated and Alone

Chapter Four 41
The Devastating Famine of Spiritual Emptiness

Chapter Five 49
Hope Lost - Dreams Dashed

Chapter Six 63
Haiti's New Generation

Chapter Seven 71
Hope Renewed – Audacious Dreams

Epilogue 77

Introduction

The mantle of leadership is a privilege accompanied by great responsibility. When leaders are chosen, they are given a mandate to accomplish the vision of those who selected them. To be successful, leaders must be given authority to make decisions and the resources necessary to fulfill the vision.

Quality of leadership cannot be measured only by the fulfillment of a mandate (quantity). Many factors determine the total or partial success/failure of a leader and the mission to which he is called. This can be answered in part by asking, "Did the leader..."

- ...effectively use the resources available?
- ...fulfill all the goals of the vision?
- ...garner support from his subordinates to the fulfillment of the tasks at hand?
- ...mentor others in leadership roles?
- ...make room for others at the top?
- ...seek advice from those with experience?

The Pearl of Leadership uses the experiences of Haiti, the world's first black republic, to illustrate the factors outlined above. Though much of Haiti's history is checkered with corruption, greed, avarice, betrayal, and poverty the nation continues to move forward. This speaks well of the majority of the people!

Haitians want to succeed. They are vitally interested in education, healthcare, self-government, prosperity and national development. What Haiti needs more than anything are leaders who look to the common good rather than their personal wealth. Haitians long for the day when hunger and poverty are in the past—a day when every citizen has enough to eat and the means to provide an income for their family.

That day is coming...sooner than the world may think! Young Haitians are rising up so their voices can be heard above the cries of destitution. These young people have a vision for their country that goes beyond the past and reaches well into the future—a vision in which Haiti will again be the "Jewel of the Antilles."

Reading this book will help you learn lessons vital to the success of any leader. Haitians have demonstrated courage and an indomitable spirit that points to the most important factor of leadership: People are the most valuable resource available! People will make or break a leader. They will help a cause succeed or will force a cause to fail. The masses, people, hold the true power.

You may not think of yourself as a leader, but the truth is that you are. Everyone has qualities of leadership and has opportunities to lead in the family, at work, in relationships and at the community level. The issue is whether you will nurture those qualities and allow them to strengthen. *The Pearl of Leadership* will help you unlock those latent qualities within and show you how to use them in a godly manner.

Chapter One

Welcome to Paradise

God saw all that He had made, and it was very good. And there was evening, and there was morning—the sixth day. (Genesis 1:31)

What is paradise? How would we know if we have found it? Some places on earth are so beautiful we can only describe them as paradise. However, is beauty the only criteria?

Join me on an imaginary journey into what has been described as paradise. Let's see what we can discover as we imagine…

- sailing on water so clear you can see 40 feet to the bottom and filled with such abundant sea life you marvel at its diversity
- discovering an island mountain range rising out of the sea so high that it can be seen from beyond the horizon

- dropping anchor at this fertile island paradise covered with lush vegetation, teeming with wildlife and watered by countless fresh-water streams
- being greeted by a people who think you have come from heaven to be with them

This is what greeted Christopher Columbus when he discovered the island known today as Hispaniola and set foot on what would become the nation of Haiti.

Hispaniola B.C. (before Columbus)

Evidence of human habitation on Hispaniola has been dated as early as 450 A.D. with the Ciboneys who migrated from today's North America. Around 900 A.D. the Tainos, members of the Arawak nation of Amazon valley origins, arrived from what is today South America.

The Tainos were a peaceful people who lived in large settlements and relied on agriculture for their sustenance. Corn was their primary crop and a staple in their diet. They also wove baskets and created useful items like the hammock. The Tainos called the island "Ayiti," which means "land of mountains."

Another people group inhabiting the island were the Caribs. Viewed as ruthless warriors by the Tainos – Carib means cannibal in the Taino language – the Caribs were known to kill their male enemies and enslave the females.

Nevertheless, Hispaniola was large enough for these competing people groups to co-exist. The lush vegetation and abundant wildlife made it possible for these early inhabitants to flourish.

Change on the Horizon

When Christopher Columbus sailed on his first voyage, his eyes were set on finding a passage to China and the Far East. When he first saw the mountains of Hispaniola rising above the distant horizon his heart must have begun pounding in his chest. After months at sea, sailing in uncharted waters, land was finally in sight. Could this be the answer to his prayers and dreams?

When Columbus anchored the Santa Maria near the coast of today's Cap-Haitien, the native Arawaks (Tainos) were delighted. Finally, help from heaven was coming that would enable them to annihilate the fierce Caribs. Though the people were disappointed that Columbus and his men were not their saviors, they still celebrated the ships arrival and helped build La Navidad, the first European settlement in the New World.

Columbus left for Spain only to return with a larger expedition of 17 ships and 1,200 Spanish soldiers

> *The Spaniards were harsh and ruthless in their domination of the native people. Today, almost no indigenous Caribbean Indians survive.*

and crew. By the time he returned to La Navidad, it had

been destroyed by the Caribs, and the Arawak and European settlers had been slaughtered. Columbus abandoned the site and moved further east on the island's north shore to establish a colony in what is now the Dominican Republic.

Gold was found near the new settlement, so the Spaniards who traveled with Columbus enslaved the native population and forced them to mine the precious metal. Leaving the Spaniards in control of Hispaniola, Columbus set sail to explore the other islands in the region.

Reign of Terror

The Spaniards were harsh and ruthless in their domination of the native people. Considered less than human, the native Taino and Carib peoples were expendable in the Spaniards' quest for riches. Less than fifty years after the first discovery of gold on Hispaniola, the Taino were completely eradicated. The Caribs fared little better. Today, almost no indigenous Carribbean Indians survive. Nevertheless, the lasting legacy of their Arawak origins can be seen in the faces of some of their Cuban and Dominican descendents.

As time passed, the cruel dynasty of greed that Columbus introduced in the New World grew ever more barbaric. Estimates place the number of Native American deaths from 300,000 to more than one million between 1492 and 1550. Most were the result of disease, but violence and suicide also took their terrible toll. In 1521 the tide of tyranny turned toward Mexico when larger gold reserves were discovered in the land of the Inca and Aztec.

Haiti Is Born

Hispaniola remained mostly unpopulated for 75 years after the Spaniards moved on to Mexico in their quest for gold. Pirates moved in, and by the year 1630 French and British Buccaneers were raiding Spanish treasure ships from a base on the island of Tortuga (Ile de la Tortue). By 1644 they had established a settlement near Port-de-Paix on the north shore of Haiti (Hispaniola).

The constant pirate raids on Spanish shipping eventually led the Crown of Spain to cede the Western third of Hispaniola to France through the Treaty of Ryswick (1697). This portion of the island was promptly renamed Saint Dominigue, later to become "La Republique d'Haiti."

Under French rule, Saint Dominigue prospered through the export of sugar, coffee, cotton, indigo, cocoa and ebony. Trade with the French colony was considered a tremendous economic success, totaling in excess of 140 million dollars.

The fertile soil and mild climate of the Caribbean contributed to the economic success of Saint Dominigue as did other factors. However, all were paled by the blight of human slavery.

Haiti's African Influence

The native inhabitants of Hispaniola had long been decimated, so there was no cheap labor to work on the plantations. To overcome this obstacle, plantation owners turned to slaves imported from Africa to fill the void. Ship after ship carrying human cargo from the Congo, Ibo, Nago, Mandingue, Arada, Dahome and other West African civilizations arrived to off-load slaves sold at markets around Haiti. To these new inhabitants, the island was a brutal place of torture, starvation, disease and back-breaking labor.

Slaves were mere commodities in the notorious Triangular Trade between Europe, Africa and the Americas.

At the dawn of the 18th century slavery was a fixture in European and Arab societies. To facilitate the export of sugar and rum to Europe, crop yield had to increase. That increase required laborers who would work for little or no payment, so slavery was the most logical choice.

Slave-raiding parties would strike in West African settlements to round-up men, women and children to be sold as slaves in the New World. These people would then be forced into the holds of slave ships, and packed so tightly together that freedom of movement was impossible and suffocation was not uncommon. Ship captains expected an average death-toll of 12 percent on their voyage across the Atlantic Ocean. Upon arrival, the survivors were fed, "oiled" and paraded through the streets to the slave market where they would be auctioned off for guns, liquor and other goods.

Slaves were mere commodities in the notorious Triangular Trade between Europe, Africa and the Americas. For countless thousands, their worth was measured in how long they could work 14+ hour days and stay alive. In fact, the average life-span of an African slave was 7 years. Many did not survive through the first year. This period of adjustment, or "seasoning" as it was called, was brutal and often fatal. Not only were these people subject to inhumane treatment, but most were separated from their families and culture, were in an unfamiliar environment, and were forced to adopt new cultural customs and language.

Slave owners required complete loyalty from their "property" and demanded their slaves sever all ties to their homeland and family. Slaves were also kept from others of their tribal or cultural background to prevent any rebellion or uprising from occurring. Nevertheless, slaves were willing to be tortured and killed if that was the price of freedom.

Seeds of Rebellion

The harsh and inhumane treatment of slaves did not go unnoticed among certain circles in both Europe and America. The recognition that slavery diminishes an entire society was gaining ground as the voices of African slaves in Europe and America were clamoring to be heard.

Likewise, the slaves of Saint Dominigue began to consider their plight in terms of numbers rather than conditions. Far more slaves inhabited Saint Dominigue than white slave-owners, so talk of an organized rebellion began to circulate. The political climate was shifting in France as well. The French Revolution took the power of government out of the hands of the aristocracy and put it into the hands of the people.

Now in Saint Dominigue, the Republican and Royalist political parties began to grow in strength and numbers. Blacks, mulattoes and whites were all vying for the power necessary to further their particular cause—maintain the status quo or freedom from slavery and corruption.

Conditions in Saint Dominigue were ripe and the winds of change were quickly growing into a howling gale. The seeds of rebellion and revolution had sprouted, grown, and now the harvest was at hand. What would come of these troubling times? Would the country survive?

Leadership Treasure #1

Potential is an opportunity facing each leader. The direction that potential flows is the leader's responsibility. Will it be for the greater good or will it bring harm and destruction? Thus leaders must treat potential with the utmost respect and honor it as a life's calling. A leader's legacy is built upon the embracing of opportunity.

Haiti teaches us that a new frontier is a test of vision and stewardship.

Tim DeTellis

Chapter Two

Haiti's Fight for Independence

My hands have made both heaven and earth, and they are mine. I, the LORD, have spoken!
Isaiah 66:2, NLT

We see pride ourselves in wearing the mask of high-spiritedness, though only You, God, are high above all. Ambition seeks honor and glory, whereas only You should be honored above all and glorified forever. The powerful man seeks to be feared, because of his cruelty, but who ought really to be feared but God alone? What can be forced away or withdrawn out of God's power? By whom, what, when or where? [1] **St. Augustine**

When left to itself, human society will naturally segregate into groups of those who have and those who

---

[1] *Confessions—St. Augustine*; Book 2, Chapter 6, p 45; Copyright © 2003, Bridge Logos

have not. Prosperity is not the norm for the majority of society as the wealth and resources are controlled by a minority of citizens in government, business or both.

Such was the case in Saint Dominigue by the year 1789. Considered to be the richest colony in the West Indies, and probably the richest in the history of the world, Saint-Domingue was blessed with fertile soil and an ideal climate. However, the harvest of this island paradise was sown and gathered by the toil, sweat and blood of slave labor. Under these conditions, the poor became poorer while the rich became richer.

Paradise Lost?

Four distinct people groups were active in Saint-Domingue when the French Revolution began in 1789, including:

- Whites (approximately 20,000 mostly French)
- Free people of color (approximately 30,000 – half of which were the mulatto children of white Frenchmen and slave women, the other half were black slaves who had purchased their freedom)
- Black slaves (approximately 500,000)
- Maroons (runaway slaves living in the mountains, keeping African customs and religion alive)

Each people group was driven by its own prevailing point of view, but also included those with competing special interests. This confusion added to the cauldron of mistrust and helped fuel the fires of discontent. Saint-Domingue was teetering precariously on the edge of revolt. Whites and free people of color were upset with the trading policies of the French motherland; other whites were furious with policies that allowed any non-whites to own land or conduct business; the black slaves were so down-trodden they needed to rise out of the mire or face sure death; the Maroons wanted Africa in the Americas. What was happening in paradise?

Rebellion of the Black Slaves

Saint-Domingue was not paradise for the black slave population. Outnumbering the whites and free people of color by a margin of ten to one, any organized uprising could have dramatic results. From the beginning, the slaves resisted and often rose in rebellion, but their attempts for freedom were quickly and harshly subdued. Nevertheless, change was in the air. Civil war in France and chaos among the whites in Saint-Domingue created a hospitable environment for the seeds of rebellion to grow.

The beginning of the massive slave rebellion that would eventually lead to their freedom and the establishment of the world's first black republic can be set on the evening of August 21, 1791. Slaves had been

> *...the floodgates holding back the rising waters of rebellion burst releasing a flood of revolution that would not recede until it covered all of Saint-Domingue...*

deserting the plantations in unprecedented numbers prior to this historic day, and as a result, the ranks of the Maroons had swelled as these runaway slaves had been assimilated into their society.

The Maroons practiced Voodoo as their primary religion, which was a throw-back to their African roots. On the evening of August 14, 1791, the Petwo Voodoo cult held a service in which a woman became possessed by the warrior spirit, Ogoun. While possessed, this woman sacrificed a black pig and then speaking in the voice of the spirit, named Boukman, Jean-Francois, Biassou and Jennot as the generals who were to lead the slaves and Maroons in a revolt against the white slave owners. These leaders were also to exact harsh judgment against the whites because of their oppression of the black slaves.

Over the following week, word spread rapidly among the slaves and the Maroons of the historic and prophetic religious service. Then, on August 21, 1791, the floodgates holding back the rising waters of rebellion burst releasing a flood of revolution that would not recede until it covered all of Saint-Domingue, and all the slaves were free.

Who Is Fighting Whom?

Early in the revolt the lines of battle were poorly drawn. The free people of color had formed a strange alliance with the black slaves, even though they tended to be more brutal slave owners than the whites. The whites didn't want to automatically issue the rights of citizens to the free people of color, but didn't want to fight against them either. Other whites demanded a change in the way France handled its trade agreement with Saint-Domingue. They wanted an agreement that was more equitable and profitable.

On September 20, 1791, a major shift on the island occurred as the Colonial Assembly authorized citizenship to all free people of color, regardless of their property and birth status. The French Assembly followed suit by granting full citizenship for free people of color on April 4, 1792. This helped galvanize the battle-lines of the Haitian revolution into slaves and Maroons on one side, whites and free people of color on the other.

An emissary from France, Leger Felicite Sonthonax, arrived in Saint-Domingue on September 18, 1792 with orders from the king to quell the uprising. Not only were the slaves in revolt, but tensions between different factions of the white minority threatened any solidarity that may be forged among them. Likewise, free people of color were still unsure of their status according to the French government.

Sonthonax felt he had accomplished his three major goals within four months of his arrival. The goals included:

- Pacification or containment of the slave rebellion
- Defeat of the primary white resistance
- Hold the colony for France

However, his accomplishments did not last. During February 1793, France declared war on Britain, which meant that Sonthonax' supply lines to France were compromised by the superior British Navy. During the same month King Louis XVI was put to death - making France a republic without a king.

With Louis XVI's death, suspicion grew toward the French government. Slaves were emboldened to pick up the rebellion, free people of color were even more unsure of their status according to the French government, and the whites were split between the royalists who demanded a king and those supporting independence.

Emancipation Looms on the Horizon

Fearing that both the British and Spanish would attack Saint-Domingue, Sonthonax began preparation for the inevitable. The French general, Galbaud, betrayed Sonthonax in an attempt to deport all the commissioners, including Sonthonax, in order to work with the British for the return of the ancient regime, thus negating any citizen status for the free men of color.

A battle ensued and it appeared that Galbaud would prevail, so Sonthonax did what he deemed necessary to quell the mutiny. He pressed 15,000 black slaves into his army to defeat Galbaud - with the promise of emancipation for serving. They agreed, with the condition that their families be freed as well. That meant 30,000 to 40,000 blacks became citizens.

Sonthonax had ignited the ire of all the whites and free men of color with his decision to emancipate the slave army used to defeat Galbaud. The remaining slaves, however, saw this as their opportunity for freedom. Sonthonax, knowing any help from the homeland was impossible with the ongoing war, decreed on August 29, 1793 the emancipation of slavery in Saint-Domingue.

The Struggle for Power

The wars with Spain and Britain brought great hardship to Saint-Domingue. Internal strife and whites who were allied with the British made it difficult to know who the enemies really were. Spain finally pulled out due to their defeat in Europe, and the British soon followed. Meanwhile, Sonthonax was summoned back to France to explain his decision to emancipate 500,000 black slaves.

The black general, Toussaint, had been the primary force to contend with from May 1794 to October 1798. During that time he had driven the British out of Saint-Domingue, had overseen the retreat of the Spanish, ousted all genuine French authority, and had become Commander-in-Chief and Governor-general of Saint-Domingue.

Toussaint continued his rise to power and became very busy brokering trade deals with France, Britain and the United States. During this time he was also working toward independence from France and leaning toward a trade agreement with the United States.

Soon another battle for Toussaint loomed with the mulatto forces under Rigaud, a former ally. Toussaint successfully defended his position and in 1801 was named governor-general for life in the new republic's constitution. He was finally arrested and returned to France where he later died.

Napoleon, who had assumed power in France, sent between 16,000 and 20,000 troops to quell the rebellion in Saint Dominigue and re-establish the colony under the more primitive rule once enjoyed there. The French businessmen who were displaced with the emancipation of the slaves, and who had lost property and commerce on the island wanted recourse, so Napoleon bowed to the pressure.

> *When slavery was restored on the island of Guadalupe in the Caribbean, Haitian leaders again rose in rebellion, determined not to go back to slavery.*

Independence Day!

When slavery was restored on the island of Guadalupe in the Caribbean, Haitian leaders again rose in rebellion, determined not to go back to slavery. During that time, Britain and France again declared war, which quickly depleted the resources necessary to re-take Haiti. Napoleon sold Louisiana to the United States to help fund the war with Britain, which meant Haiti no longer held strategic importance for France. Therefore, to avoid depleting French resources further, Napoleon refused to send any military support to the French commander in Haiti. The French commander then fled to Jamaica, and Haiti went under the control of Jean-Jacque Dessalines, a former field slave.

Haiti formally declared independence from France on January 1, 1804, becoming the world's first black republic. In 1805, Dessalines declared himself Emperor of Haiti hearkening the beginning of a new era for the Pearl of the Antilles.

At What Cost?

What was the cost of Haiti's independence? How can one even count the true cost of 13 years of war?

The new nation's infrastructure was completely in shambles. The prevailing attitude of the revolutionary warriors was to eradicate all European influences from Haiti - including the plantations, factories, and holdings of the slave owners.

Untold thousands had lost their lives or loved ones to violence, disease and disaster. The shear brutality of acts committed by both sides goes beyond rational human conscience. Each side traded atrocity with atrocity, the descriptions of which are sickening and beyond belief - even to those accustomed to human brutality toward others. The last year of the Haitian Revolution was as savage as any conflict one can read of in human history. It truly became a war of racial extermination on both sides.

With no clear vision for the future, the new nation spent the next 100 years in utter turmoil, as natural resources were depleted and leaders marched in and out of office. The revolt began in a Voodoo service as a demon spoke through a woman and named officers of the fledgling black army. By virtue of that "prophecy" alone, the entire effort was handed over to Satan to use the men and women of Haiti as he desired to bring about his ungodly purposes. Jesus said:

> *"The thief comes only to steal and kill and destroy; I have come that they may have life, and have it to the full."* (John 10:10)

Will Haiti choose life?

Leadership Treasure #2

The greatest war a leader faces is the fight against self-centered vision that looms larger than concern for others. Concern for self over others leads to destructive decisions that bring harm to those under the leader's care.

Haiti teaches us that a war fueled by greed results in death.

Chapter Three

Isolated and Alone

He sent darkness and made the land dark—
for had they not rebelled against his words?
(Psalms 105:28)

The immoral blight of slavery drew Saint-Domingue into the throes of revolution. After thirteen years of violence and inhumane bloodshed, a new nation was born…Haiti, the world's first black republic.

As the fledgling nation sought to bring stability to its war-torn countryside, competing interests within the revolutionary ranks led to in-fighting and even more violence. One leader wanted to establish a kingdom with him as king. Another wanted a free, democratic government similar to the United States to the north. Yet another looked to the pattern of France and sought to establish a black aristocracy that enjoyed privileges not available to the common masses.

For the vast majority of Haitians, the establishment of government was eclipsed by the daily struggle to survive. Freedom, while far superior to the inhumane slavery they had experienced, presented new and different challenges to overcome. Sadly, Haiti would learn that slavery comes in many forms - each of which leads to death.

To Whom Do We Turn

The call to battle was received during a Voodoo ritual in August of 1791. During that service, a woman became possessed by Ogoun, the warrior spirit, and then named the generals who would lead the revolt. The revolution was conceived and the new nation birthed under the darkness of occult, Voodoo worship. This same darkness became a shroud that descended over the land and dulled the minds of the people. Their eyes were not focused on God, but on evil, satanic rituals and idol worship.

Jesus said:

> *Your eye is a lamp for your body. A pure eye lets sunshine into your soul. But an evil eye shuts out the light and plunges you into darkness. If the light you think you have is really darkness, how deep that darkness will be!* (Matt. 6:22-23 NLT)

The conditions Jesus described were embodied in the nation of Haiti as they rushed headlong into a new era ill-equipped to handle the stress and strain of forming a nation. A parallel can be drawn with the formation of another nation whose story is told in the Bible.

The children of Israel were slaves in the nation of Egypt for more than 400 years. Finally, conditions became so brutal that they cried out to God for freedom. God heard their cry, saw their terror, and He called upon Moses to lead them out.

Moses faced many trials as he confronted the Egyptian king about setting Israel free. Ten brutal plagues, the last of which claimed all the firstborn of Egypt, finally forced the king to release the people to their freedom. Then, following Moses, they fled into the deserts of Sinai.

The need for God's help to lead the people weighed heavily on Moses, so he continually cried out to God in prayer for guidance and understanding. However, the people groaned and grumbled about the conditions they encountered living in the desert. This culminated with their building a golden calf to worship.

When Moses discovered the treachery he cried out to God for mercy, knowing that judgment would follow such a grievous act. That day, more than 3,000 people were killed in an earthquake followed quickly by a deadly plague. Only when the people repented did their fortunes turn.

One form of slavery was broken when the children of Israel left Egypt.

> *God had been introduced to the island, but those who introduced Him did not demonstrate the integrity of true Christian witness.*

Nevertheless, another form of slavery lay in wait in the vast barrenness of Sinai, seeking to overwhelm the people and return them to bondage.

Let Freedom Ring?

If you do what is right, will you not be accepted? But if you do not do what is right, sin is crouching at your door; it desires to have you, but you must master it. (Gen. 4:7)

God's words to Cain reflect the truth that confronted Haiti. Sin indeed crouches at the door, waiting to overwhelm us and bind us in sin. Scripture clearly teaches that bondage to sin is a form of slavery, and sin is what engulfed Haiti through Voodoo rites and satanic worship rituals. God had been introduced to the island, but those who introduced Him did not demonstrate the integrity of true Godly witness. Therefore, the Africans who were brought there as slaves held on to their ancient pagan religion and were again bound over to the darkness and slavery of sin.

Immediately after independence, Dessalines declared himself Emperor of Haiti and sought to create a court. Though his efforts were met with ridicule by the more educated mulattoes, Dessalines did promote certain others to create an aristocracy while reserving royalty for himself. He also encouraged marriages between the black and mulatto factions, though the offer of his daughter to Alexandre Petion was rejected.

Economically, Haiti was in ruins. To revive production of goods, Dessalines attempted to re-introduce forced labor on the plantations. This effort failed, as did his effort to secure control of the Spanish eastern side of Hispaniola. The self-proclaimed emperor was eventually assassinated and Haiti was again on the hunt for a leader.

Two strong contenders emerged, Henri Christophe and Alexandre Petion. The mulatto elite selected Christophe, a black general, to be president and Petion to serve as head of the legislature. The elite controlled Christophe and assumed that other stand-in black leaders would follow his leadership.

This was not to be. Christophe marched on Port-au-Prince, but his military action failed. Petion had fortified the city and using the artillery that Christophe lacked, was able to thwart the attack. Christophe then marched north and captured Cap Haitien, declaring himself King Henry I of Haiti and renaming the city to Cap Henry. Christophe then brought in warriors from Dahoumey in Central Africa to serve as his elite guard. Meanwhile, Petion was chosen by the elite to be President-for-Life of the Republic of Haiti and setup office in the capital city, Port-au-Prince.

King Henry I (Christophe) and President-for-Life, Petion, had very different ideologies regarding government. Christophe kept the plantations intact and the former slaves could not leave them. Though free men, they were not at liberty to do as they wished.

Nevertheless, working conditions were easier and each worker received one quarter of the crop as wages.

King Henry's rule was severe, but as export production improved, so did the standard of living. However, the king could not do without a palace so he sacrificed between 10,000 and 20,000 lives to build San Souci and the citadel, La Ferriere.

Petion, in the spirit of the French Revolution, divided the land in the south into small parcels to facilitate the creation of a society of free yeomen. His soldiers received the parcels free while others paid a small price. This policy enabled each family to produce food for their own consumption, but did not lend itself to building any export earnings to pay for imports. Without sugar cane production in the south, the sugar mills and other subsidiary enterprises were forced to close.

Petion was widely respected and honored when he died in 1818, and was succeeded by General Jean-Pierre Boyer, one of his aides. King Henry eventually suffered a stroke and committed suicide rather than face harsh treatment by his subjects. Upon Henry's death, Boyer led an army north and captured Cap Haitien, thus reuniting Haiti.

Boyer's leadership did little for the Haitian economy and it stagnated under his rule. To further complicate matters, Boyer made a large payment to the French government to secure final acceptance of Haitian independence. This, coupled with a stagnant economy, caused conditions in Haiti to deteriorate even more, leading to an eventual rebellion to remove him from office.

Throughout the 19th century and into the 20th century, Haiti struggled under factious leaders, each carving out a huge slice for themselves and leaving little for the citizens. Two political parties emerged, the National Party, controlled by blacks and the Liberal Party, controlled by the mulattos.

In 1915 General Guillaume Sam gained the presidency and immediately had 167 political prisoners

> *Ending the bloodshed was the official cause of the U.S. occupation of Haiti from 1915-1934.*

executed. This incited a massive riot in Port-au-Prince causing Sam to flee to the French embassy for safety. The mob broke through the French defenses and took Sam away. The rioters then tore Sam to pieces and paraded his dismembered body through the streets. This total breakdown of law and order was used as justification for United States forces to occupy Haiti.

Ending the bloodshed was the official cause of the U.S. occupation of Haiti. Haiti's location in the Caribbean Sea enabled U.S. forces to keep watch on the Panama Canal and protect U.S. interests in keeping the Canal open. The U.S. occupation lasted from 1915 through 1934 during which time considerable infrastructure was put in place.

Upon the withdrawal of U.S. troops, Rafael Trujillo Molina, Commander of the Army in the Dominican Republic came into control of the Dominican Republic. His interests spanned beyond the eastern two-thirds of Hispaniola and spilled over into Haiti. To that end,

Trujillo sent spies and agents into Haiti to help him reach his goals. Though Trujillo had aspirations of controlling the entire island, Haiti remained an independent republic and rebuffed Trujillo's designs.

Another man on the list of dictators was Francois Duvalier, a medical doctor who won a free and open election for the presidency. Though Duvalier, "Papa Doc," was the legitimate winner of the election, he had no scruples regarding his use of power and force to remain in office. He ruled Haiti from 1957 until 1971, using fear, torture and death to have his way. The "tonton makouts," Duvalier's execution squads, roamed the Haitian countryside killing anyone who opposed the dictator.

Francois Duvalier died in 1971 and leadership passed to his son, Jean-Claude Duvalier, "Baby Doc." Jean-Claude did not share his father's taste for ruling as much as his taste for luxury. To feed his insatiable lust for riches, Baby Doc used corruption and theft.

> *Hardwoods that were once plentiful have been decimated for use as charcoal, the primary cooking fuel used in Haiti.*

The Duvalier's reign exacted an enormous toll on Haitian society. It is estimated that 50,000 Haitians were executed during the reign of Papa Doc and Baby Doc. Finally, in 1986 the Duvalier's reign of terror ended.

What Is Next?

With the Duvalier's gone, a new era has settled upon Haiti. Now, more than ever, Haiti is at a crossroads. Corrupt leadership and failed economic programs have left an island paradise denuded of the hardwoods that once flourished on its fertile hillsides, and is devastated by floods and mudslides. The waters surrounding Haiti do not have enough aquatic life to sustain any fishing enterprises and exports are out of the question. Sadly, Haitian fishermen barely catch enough for their families to eat, let alone enough for a village or a country.

Hardwoods that were once plentiful have been decimated for use as charcoal, the primary cooking fuel used in Haiti. As these trees are cut down and burned into charcoal, the topsoil is exposed to erosion by wind and rain. As each hurricane season comes and goes, more of Haiti is washed out to sea, never to be recovered.

People have little vision for the future when their lives are consumed with the need to survive. Thus is the condition of Haiti. Though people know their activities are harmful (charcoal production, over fishing, etc.), the need to feed their families takes a much higher priority. So the questions must be asked:

- What is the answer?
- To whom do we turn?

The message is very close at hand; it is on your lips and in your heart so that you can obey it. (Deut. 30:14 NLT)

Leadership Treasure #3

God-inspired vision frees leaders and motivates them to greatness. Self-centered vision enslaves leaders and results in eventual destruction. To be truly free is to know that your identity is found in Christ alone. Without the anchor of Christ, a leader's life is like a ship without a captain - wandering aimlessly, tossed about by the wind and waves.

Haiti teaches us that man's vision often leads to the exploitation of others to fulfill the dream.

Chapter Four

The Devastating Famine of Spiritual Emptiness

*"I will hide My face from them," [the LORD]
said, "and see what their end will be; for they
are a perverse generation, children who are
unfaithful…They made Me jealous by what is
no god and angered Me with their worthless
idols…I will send wasting famine against
them, consuming pestilence and deadly
plague…"* (Deuteronomy 32:20-21, 24 NIV)

The people of Haiti were determined to exist as a
sovereign nation in the world. Memory of the sacrifices
made during the years of revolution reinforced their
resolve and kept them looking for the right leader to
guide them.

One after another, leaders came and went. To judge
their hearts is not our purpose, but examination of the

fruit of their administrations reveals failure after failure on the part of these men. None were able to break the yoke of poverty that threatened to crush the people.

We have already seen how the land had been stripped bare and the surrounding ocean depleted of fish. Unrestrained cutting of the lush forests for charcoal production have left the Haitian countryside a barren, erosion-scarred landscape filled with people who barely get by from day-to-day. Runoff filled with the island's soil chokes the rivers and spills into the sea laden with silt. This endless cycle alters the delicate balance of life in the sea so that fishermen no longer have fish to catch and families go hungry.

Corrupt leaders intent on lining their pockets with gold have contributed to the desolation of Haiti as well. When the vision of the leader is to take what he wants when he wants it, the people suffer. Ultimately, it is the people who pay for the excesses of the leaders, but is this the only reason Haiti is so bound to poverty? Is this why the people suffer so?

Spiritual Poverty vs. Physical Poverty

We have already learned that the leaders of the revolution received the directive to go to war from a "warrior" spirit in the midst of a Voodoo ritual. The very act of reaching out to these spirits acknowledges them above God and His Son, Jesus Christ. Instead of depending on God's Holy Spirit to guide and direct, Haitian leaders depended upon ungodly spirits for leadership.

The Scripture quoted at the beginning of this chapter shows God's attitude toward the Children of Israel when they abandoned Him and sought guidance from the gods of Egypt. God hid His face from them and turned them over to all the sadness, misery and depravity that ungodliness brings.

Israel's disobedience led to spiritual poverty that surpassed anything they had ever experienced as slaves in Egypt. They had lost their vision of God as their Provider, Sustainer and Redeemer and had turned to the worship of demons:

They made Him jealous with their foreign gods and angered Him with their detestable idols. They sacrificed to demons, which are not God... (Deut. 32:16, 17)

God knew that the idols of their false worship would not, and could not save Israel, and His anger burned as He considered their rebellion:

Now where are their gods, the rock they took refuge in, the gods who ate the fat of their sacrifices and drank the wine of their drink offerings? Let them rise up to help you! Let them give you shelter! (Deut. 32:37-38)

Israel was beginning to learn that spiritual poverty leads to physical poverty. They began to realize that a nation who turns away from God never will prosper.

Their only choice was to turn again to God in repentance, declaring Him as their Sovereign Lord in order to take hold of His promises:

If you fully obey the LORD your God and carefully follow all his commands I give you today, the LORD your God will set you high above all the nations on earth. All these blessings will come upon you and accompany you if you obey the LORD your God: You will be blessed in the city and blessed in the country.

The fruit of your womb will be blessed, and the crops of your land and the young of your livestock—the calves of your herds and the lambs of your flocks.

Your basket and your kneading trough will be blessed. You will be blessed when you come in and blessed when you go out.

The LORD will grant that the enemies who rise up against you will be defeated before you. They will come at you from one direction but flee from you in seven.

The LORD will send a blessing on your barns and on everything you put your hand to. The

LORD your God will bless you in the land he is giving you.

The LORD will establish you as his holy people, as he promised you on oath, if you keep the commands of the LORD your God and walk in his ways.

Then all the peoples on earth will see that you are called by the name of the LORD, and they will fear you.

The LORD will grant you abundant prosperity--in the fruit of your womb, the young of your livestock and the crops of your ground--in the land he swore to your forefathers to give you.

The LORD will open the heavens, the storehouse of his bounty, to send rain on your land in season and to bless all the work of your hands. You will lend to many nations but will borrow from none.

The LORD will make you the head, not the tail. If you pay attention to the commands of the LORD your God that I give you this day and carefully follow them, you will always be at the top, never at the bottom.
(Deut. 28:1-13)

Spiritual Emptiness

Early Haitian leaders believed the lies of Voodoo spirits - demons who wanted to destroy both them and the land. They were blinded to the fact that the promises given to Israel so many centuries before were for them as well. Their minds were darkened to the fact that God wants Haiti to be blessed and to be prosperous.

> *Early Haitian leaders believed the lies of Voodoo spirits, demons who wanted to destroy both them and the land.*

The emptiness in Haiti's depleted natural resources mirrors the condition of the souls of the nation's greatest resource, the people. Spiritual malnourishment is rampant in a nation of desperate people looking for something, but they don't know what...or who.

Haiti entered 100 years of isolation after the revolution and experienced a push back to the tribal life of their African heritage. This brought about a period of deep starvation - the likes of which the people had never before experienced. The devastation of natural resources resulted from this starvation of the soul as people began

> *Haitians became desperate for any change that would make their lives better and bring stability to their country.*

to take desperate measures to better their physical lives. This in turn caused the quality of life for everyone to diminish and brought with it new, greater levels of hopelessness.

The axiom that desperate people do desperate things is true as is evidenced by the increasing despair in the nation of Haiti at the dawn of the 20th Century. "What has freedom brought to us?" was the cry of countless Haitians as they struggled to feed themselves and their families. "What is the meaning of an existence filled with hunger, disease and death?"

Yet the sacrifices to demons continued. Allegiance to false gods increased. Syncretism, the blending of Christian and Voodoo beliefs, became ever more idolatrous. How far would Haiti fall before she hit bottom?

Is There a Doctor in the House?

Haitians became desperate for any change that would make their lives better and bring stability to their country. They knew their nation was ill and in need of radical treatments to bring it to the point where families could move beyond mere survival and flourish.

Inside this boiling cauldron of hopelessness and despair a young country doctor began treating yaws, a vicious tropical disease that eats away the victims' flesh, much like leprosy. "Papa Doc," as the people lovingly called him, traveled the length and breadth of the land treating the poor and helping them overcome the dreaded disease.

The Haitian elite looked down upon the peasants and considered them unworthy of medical care. However, Dr. Francois Duvalier, driven by an event he witnessed years earlier, worked tirelessly treating the poor and eradicating yaws from the land of Haiti. This simple country doctor was credited with saving hundreds of thousands of lives across the land, endearing him in the hearts and minds of the population.

Little did these simple folk know what impact Dr. Francois Duvalier would have on their lives and the life of their nation. How could anyone know the nightmare would unfold in just a few short years?

Leadership Treasure #4

The roots of a tree determine its growth. If the roots are withered and dry, the tree suffers. If the roots are deep in fertile soil and well watered, the tree will flourish. Likewise, a leader's roots determine his growth. The depth of his faith, the place of his hope, and the master he serves seals the leader's fate (2 Cor. 3:23).

Haiti teaches us that we can only serve one master.

Chapter Five

Hope Lost - Dreams Dashed

You will not be given a proper burial, for you have destroyed your nation and slaughtered your people... (Isaiah 14:20 NLT)

To know even one life has breathed easier because you have lived. This is to have succeeded. Ralph Waldo Emerson

What is the measure of success? How one answers that question determines the course of their life and affects their attitude toward others who either help or hinder their progress. The size of an amassed fortune; the quantity and quality of accumulated goods; the power one has over another; reaching the highest levels of government or business? Or is it as Emerson said in the quote above, "To know even one life has breathed easier because you have lived"?

Cauldron of Discontent

Francois Duvalier was born in a Haiti that increasingly struggled to feed its hungry masses. The age-old struggle between whites, mulattos and blacks showed no sign of abating and the poor became even poorer.

One day in 1924 when Duvalier was a teenager he watched as a man and three women held a struggling child while his mother scrubbed at the running sores covering his little body. The mother scrubbed despite the child's cries, her own face twisted in a pain that only mothers can understand. Her little baby was infected with yaws, a terrible flesh-eating disease that was rampant across the Haitian countryside.

That day, while Duvalier watched in silence, he decided to become a doctor so he could help those in the most need. True to his vow, Francois Duvalier graduated from medical school in July of 1934.

Immediately, Duvalier began to work to help alleviate the pain of those inflicted with yaws. To him, this was the most pressing crisis facing the Haitian population, especially among the rural poor.

> *Duvalier dreamed of Haiti being free of foreign influence and governed by the black majority.*

Another factor that shaped young Duvalier was the U.S. occupation of Haiti from 1915-1934. Though much-needed infrastructure was built and stability in government was brought to the national countryside, Haitians resented the white soldiers and wanted them to leave their nation. The United States wanted to bring stability to the island nation, but also wanted to have a military presence near the Panama Canal to prevent any interference with free passage by Nazi Germany.

Duvalier dreamed of Haiti being free of foreign influence and governed by the black majority. He yearned for the day when black voices could be heard and power was taken from hands of the wealthy elite and put into the hands of the people. To that end, he completely supported a man who promised such a black revolution, Dumarsais Estimé.

Estimé, scrupulously honest in the midst of corruption, was elected to the presidency after a military junta deposed Elie Lescot. His campaign ran on the platform of putting a black man in power and running the government with honesty and integrity. After decades of white and mulatto rule, this proved to be a successful strategy. His presidency saw the blacks elevated in business, and government no longer relegated to minor or insignificant roles. For a time, the blacks enjoyed prosperity and saw their condition improve, but again corruption overtook the positive gains. Though Estimé was never implicated in any scandals, he was still deposed by an army coup and former army colonel, Paul Magloire, assumed the presidency.

For Duvalier, this was a tragedy. He discovered that the army had enough power to make or break a presidency, so his mistrust of them grew exponentially. This seed of mistrust began to germinate in Duvalier, later to grow into the most vile, brutal, lawless, government-sanctioned body in Haitian history.

During this same time, both the Catholic and Protestant churches in Haiti stepped up their campaign to outlaw the Voodoo religion. With fiery rhetoric, clergy denounced the practice of Voodoo and the priests (houngans) who officiated at the Voodoo ceremonies. These tactics did not sit well with black Haitians, who resented white European priests telling them how to worship. Religion in Haiti had long been subject to syncretism with the blending of Voodoo and Catholic/Christian deity and worship.

Duvalier, who had been on the fringe as far as Voodoo was concerned, now devoured all he could learn about the religion. His studies carried him deep into the traditional beliefs of Voodoo and the spirits (loas) who were worshiped. As his interest grew, his hunger for more became insatiable. The stage was being set and the players being assembled for a new black "revolution."

Papa Doc

The tropical disease, yaws, had risen to epidemic proportions during the 1940's with nearly 75 percent of the Haitian population infected. Caused by a bacteria of the same family that causes syphilis, relapsing fever and other diseases, yaws is also highly contagious. During 1943, the Inter-American Affairs Commission sent Dr. James Dwinelle to Haiti to analyze the situation and find local doctors to work in rural clinics where the disease was most prevalent. One of those interviewed was Dr. Francois Duvalier.

Dr. Dwinelle hired Duvalier and placed him at the Rural Clinic of Gressier, 15 miles southwest of Port-Au-Prince, the most yaws-infected area of the nation. Diverted from his obsession with Voodoo, Duvalier immersed himself completely into curing the masses using penicillin treatments. His success was such that various international medical journals published the results of his research. "Papa Doc," as he was lovingly called by hundreds of thousands of his patients, had hit his stride.

When Estimé became president, he tapped Duvalier on the shoulder to serve as his Under Secretary of Labor and later as the Public Health and Labor Minister. The black revolution begun by Estimé reinforced Duvalier's belief that the only way to solve the racial problems in Haiti was to reopen the bloody conflict between blacks and mulattos in order to break their ruling class structure. To drive his point home, Duvalier, along with Lorimer Denis, wrote *The Problem of Classes Throughout Haiti's History*. The political side of Duvalier was beginning to emerge.

> *Duvalier believed that the only way to solve the racial problems in Haiti was to reopen the bloody conflict between blacks and mulattos in order to break their ruling class structure.*

President for Life, Francois Duvalier

By May of 1956, four candidates had announced their decision to run in an election to replace out-going president, Paul Magloire. The candidates included, Clément Jumelle, Daniel Fignolé, Louis Déjoie and "Papa Doc" Francois Duvalier. Through a long and dangerous campaign, Duvalier insisted that black Haiti be governed by blacks. Because of his work throughout the rural areas eradicating yaws, Papa Doc was loved and even revered by the people. Garnering this grass-roots support, Duvalier won the election on September 22, 1956 with a staggering majority of 679,884 votes compared to Déjoie's 266,992; the other two candidates had dropped out of the race.

From the beginning of Duvalier's reign, he set out to rid himself of his enemies and opponents. One-by-one they were eliminated by intimidation, imprisonment, torture or death. Also among the first acts of the new president was the emasculation of the army. Duvalier knew that the army could remove him from office, so he created an invincible force of civilians called the Volunteers of National Security (VSN), commonly called the Tonton Macoutes. This armed civilian militia was responsible only to the president and stood above even the army and police. Mostly comprised of illiterate peasants, the VSN was virulent in their loyalty to His Excellency and would do anything, including torture and murder to forward the president's agenda. The VSN became a feared and hated enemy of the people over the next three decades of Duvalier rule.

Duvalier's obsession with Voodoo continued to grow deeper. His wife, Simone, was deeply immersed in the religion as well, and had been all her life. Duvalier knew that to gain complete mastery over the people, he needed Haiti's most powerful spirits to always be at his side. To accomplish this he went to the cave, Trou Foban, known since the time of slavery as the home of evil spirits who had roamed the countryside until they gathered there and settled. The place was greatly feared because of the supernatural might of the spirits that inhabited its depths. Only the most powerful houngans could conjure these spirits because they were nothing to be taken lightly.

Confident in his mission, Duvalier and a houngan trekked to the cave and began a ceremony to invite the spirits who lived there to move into a special room built for them in the

> *Duvalier knew that to gain complete mastery over the people, he needed Haiti's most powerful spirits to always be at his side.*

palace. The ceremony lasted until well into the night, but ended successfully as the spirits accompanied Duvalier back to the palace and took up residence there. They remained with him until he died, and because of them came the legend that no human being could ever overthrow him.

The reign of terror propagated by Francois Duvalier lasted until his death, but Duvalierism (a totalitarian dictatorship) lasted long after through his son, Jean-

Claude. When the Duvaliers saw something they wanted, they took it. If someone was in their way, they were removed—alive or dead, it didn't matter.

Conniving, shrewd, suspicious, violent, sadistic and immoral acts occurred in the palace on a daily basis. A special room painted blood red was used to interrogate and torture prisoners. Often, the president would sit and peer through a peephole to watch as torture was administered. Other times, he would listen to tapes of the torture and find special joy in the groans and cries of the person being tortured. Thus the enigma of Papa Doc - savior of hundreds of thousands during the yaws epidemic; torturer and slayer of tens of thousands during his presidential reign.

April 21, 1971

Finally, on April 21, 1971, the heart of Francois Duvalier gave out and Haiti entered a new chapter of corruption, greed and apathetic indifference to the needs of the people. Papa Doc was dead, but his successor had already been designated, Jean-Claude Duvalier, the president's son.

The day of Francois' funeral marked a transition that few could have foreseen. Francois was intimately in tune with all the workings of the government and made decisions on every detail; Jean-Claude had no interest in the government and was ill-prepared to be its head.

As the funeral procession wound through the streets of Port-Au-Prince to the cemetery, a heavily sedated Jean-Claude remained in the palace. Suddenly, a fierce whirlwind that originated on the palace grounds followed the same route as the funeral procession to the cemetery. Terrified Haitians scrambled to get out of the way of the horrendous wind, believing that the spirits Duvalier had brought to live with him were accompanying him to the cemetery. On that day Haitians believed those same spirits entered the body of Francois' son, Jean-Claude. The legacy would continue through a new President-for-Life.

Jean-Claudism

The new president was not political. Instead, he was the son of a workaholic dictator who resented his father's absence and lack of fatherly leadership. Jean-Claude found solace with his friends at parties where alcohol, drugs and women were freely available. His only interests were partying, riding motorcycles, and racing cars. Obesity did not seem to hamper this hard-living playboy, but then he didn't have to work for a living like others in Haiti.

When Jean-Claude assumed the presidency, his interests remained the same. Instead of attending to matters of State, he left it up to the Cabinet. If pressure mounted in a certain area, he would fire the Cabinet Minister responsible and replace them with someone else. This revolving-door of cabinet-level

> *The money sent to Haiti for humanitarian aid and infrastructure repair rarely, if ever, found its intended target.*

ministers did little to engender confidence in his government.

Jean-Claude's primary governmental interest was bringing in millions of dollars of aid from other countries, especially the United States to the north. Like his father, Jean-Claude played the anti-communist hand like a pro. With communist Cuba next door, the U.S. welcomed a friendly voice in the region, despite the shortcomings of the regime in place.

The money sent to Haiti for humanitarian aid and infrastructure repair/construction rarely, if ever, found its intended target. Instead, Jean-Claude's Minister of Finance would squirrel the funds away in Swiss bank accounts for the president's personal use. Other funding would be used to pay-off corrupt officials in both the U.S. and Haiti, ensuring the flow of dollars would continue.

Meanwhile, the country's slide into the abyss of hunger and despair gained momentum. Unable to feed herself, Haiti depended upon outside sources for the most basic food items. Starvation under Jean-Claude grew to new levels, and hungry Haitians became the new bargaining chip for him to use to squeeze additional aid monies out of wealthy neighboring countries, especially the U.S.

As the country spiraled downward, the people turned to desperate measures to ensure their survival. Mothers resorted to infanticide because there was not enough food to raise another child. Men worked like slaves in the sugarcane fields of the Dominican Republic to try and feed their starving families. Entire forests were stripped bare and the wood turned to charcoal to be sold as cooking fuel.

The country was in dire straits and the people were becoming increasingly restless. Jean-Claude's mother, Simone, remembered the pact her husband made with the devil 22 years earlier - ensuring his reign would be supreme. Twenty-two was a magic number in Duvalierism Voodoo so it was time to renew the pact. The problem was that the spirits would not honor Jean-Claude because he was too young, and Simone could not enter the pact on Jean-Claude's behalf, as his mother. The only way Simone could renew the pact with the devil was to do so as Jean-Claude's wife.

On September 22, 1979 in a ritualistic Voodoo ceremony that was validated at Catholic masses around the nation, Simone and Jean-Claude were wed. Once this was done, Simone, as Haiti's First Lady, contacted the devil on behalf of her President-for-Life "husband" and negotiated a renewed pact that would last until September 22, 2001.

The New First Lady

Into this world of corruption and wanton debauchery came a new force to be reckoned with, Michèle Bennett, Jean-Claude's future wife. Introduced at a party by one of Jean-Claude's friends, Michèle and the president immediately fell in love. Finally Jean-Claude had found someone who could satisfy his insatiable lust.

Ms. Bennett was not without a history. She and Jean-Claude had gone to the same school as children and he was fascinated with her then - even though at age 12 Michèle had a reputation among the boys. Her father was not keen on the idea of her having any kind of relationship with Duvalier's son.

When Michèle re-entered Jean-Claude's life, she blew in like the fierce storms that sweep across the denuded Haitian landscape. She was beautiful, petite, strong, outspoken, and the object of Jean-Claude's complete affection. Therefore, Michèle got anything and eveything she wanted.

What especially caught her eye was the position of First Lady. All she needed to do was marry the president and move Simone out of the way. Their engagement was announced much to the displeasure of the public. Michèle was divorced with children, which was anathema to Haitian mores. Added to the public outcry was the disapproval of Simone and her mother. How presumptuous of this coarse, promiscuous, foul-mouthed mulatto that she could become the wife of President-for-Life Jean-Claude Duvalier!

> *When Michèle re-entered Jean-Claude's life, she blew in like the fierce storms that sweep across the denuded Haitian landscape.*

Despite all this, Jean-Claude and Michèle were married on May 27, 1980. Their wedding was an over-the-top, extravagant affair that cost the starving people of Haiti $3,000,000. This day was more than a wedding date; it was also the beginning of the end for Jean-Claude and Duvalierism.

Michèle threw herself into the role of First Lady with all her vigor. Imagining herself something of a Haitian Evita Durate, Argentina's most hated, most loved First Lady. In this role, she founded a hospital for pregnant women and their babies. Sadly, this very project became one of the most foul places in Haiti, as the conditions there were filthy and disease-ridden. Later, it became a cocaine warehouse for Michèle's drug-running family members.

Duvalierism's Downfall

Meanwhile the drugs, parties and extravagant expenses continued. Untold millions of dollars were taken from the nation's coffers and deposited into the Duvalier's personal holdings. Human-rights violations were commonplace, as were murders, coercion, torture and death by starvation in the prisons.

By late 1985, Jean-Claude's hold on the nation was crumbling. Conditions were so bad that the silent masses finally began to riot in search of an end to their continual, gnawing hunger. As the violence spread, governments surrounding Haiti began to lobby for the president to resign and leave so that democratic elections could be held. The U.S. began to withhold vital aid money and supply shipments were drastically cut.

Finally, on February 7, 1986, Jean-Claude could hang on no longer. He, Michèle, their children, Simone and other family members boarded a U.S. Air Force jet and left the island nation. Duvalierism had come to an end, leaving in its wake a devastated and destitute nation filled with starving people. The dream of the world's first black republic being governed by blacks was shattered.[2]

Leadership Treasure #5

A leader's greatest dream should be to help solve the problems of others; to help fulfill their dreams, not his alone.

When the dream is all about you, you will miss its power. Your answer to the question, *"How do I help others live better?"* will expose your dream.

Haiti teaches us that God's dream is not about us, but those that He loves.

---

[2] For an excellent treatise on the years of Duvalier rule in Haiti, I recommend the book, *Haiti: The Duvaliers and Their Legacy*, by Elizabeth Abbott, © copyright 1988, McGraw-Hill Book Company.

Chapter Six

Haiti's New Generation

*Even when I am old and gray, do not forsake
me, O God, till I declare your power to the
next generation, your might to all who are to
come.* (Psalms 71:18 NIV)

The departure of Jean-Claude Duvalier in the spring
of 1986, and the subsequent collapse of his government,
left a vacuum of leadership that had to be filled. General
Henri Namphy stepped in as the new President of Haiti
and began to work sorting out the mess left by the
Duvalier's.

The provisional government remained in place until
1990 when Jean-Bertrand Aristide was democratically
elected. The nation remained in turmoil, however, as
Aristide was soon deposed by a coup and sought asylum
in the United States. Meanwhile, conditions among the
poor continued to deteriorate. Hunger was rampant
while the nation's infrastructure continued to crumble
under the strain.

The people wanted power, but were powerless to get it. Education held the key, but in Haiti, education is very costly. Change was inevitable, but what kind? Francois Duvalier promised change through a black revolution, but the stated promises and dreams of results never materialized. In their place were corruption, greed, brutality, starvation and death.

Into this void Haiti's next generation began to form. Not satisfied with empty promises and unfulfilled dreams, this new Haiti began to emerge. Birthing pains are not pleasant, neither is the uncertainty of tomorrow, but returning to the old Duvalierism was out of the question.

History of Education in Haiti

Haitians knew from the beginning after independence that education held the key to their future success. This knowledge led the writers of the 1805 constitution to include a provision for free and compulsory primary education. By 1820 there were nineteen primary schools and three secondary schools. The Education Act of 1848 created rural primary schools with a more limited curriculum and established colleges of medicine and law.

Despite these government actions no effective educational system was developed, which caused the emerging elite in the cities to send their children to school in France. Meanwhile, though education was provided for in the constitution, the rural peasants and the poor remained illiterate.

The year 1860 saw the signing of a Concordat with the Vatican, which resulted in the arrival of clerical teachers. This further emphasized the influence of the Roman Catholic Church in the lives of the educated class. These Roman Catholic schools essentially became nonsecular public schools jointly funded by the Haitian government and the Vatican.

The Roman Catholic schools typically employed French clergy, which in turn promoted an attachment to France in the classrooms. These clerical teachers concentrated on educating the elite in the cities where most of the schools were located. They also promoted the greatness of France and denigrated Haiti for its backward condition and lack of capacity for self-rule. The curriculum consisted primarily of literature and memorization, and remained mostly unchanged until the 1980's. Vocational schools were started during the U.S. occupation (1915-1934), but were resisted by the elites. Upon U.S. withdrawal in 1934, the government restored the old system.

Enrollment in both primary and secondary schools increased during the 1970's and 1980's, especially in the cities. Though administrative and curriculum reforms

> *Education remains beyond the means of most Haitians who are unable to afford the supplemental fees, school supplies, and uniforms required.*

were instituted during the regime of Jean-Claude Duvalier, as of 1982 about 65 percent of the population over ten years of age had received no education, and only 8 percent were educated beyond the primary level.

Education remains beyond the means of most Haitians who are unable to afford the supplemental fees, school supplies, and uniforms required. Reform measures, especially the use of Haitian Creole, have also met resistance. Thus, education remains a privilege of the upper and middle classes, with fluency in French a marker of success.

Due to weak governmental provision of education services, private and parochial schools account for about 90 percent of primary schools, and only 65 percent of primary school-aged children are actually enrolled. At the secondary level, the figure drops to around 20 percent. Less than 35 percent of those who enter will complete primary school. Although Haitians place a high value on education, few can afford to send their children to secondary school. Today, primary school enrollment is dropping due to economic factors. Sixty percent of rural households suffer from chronic food shortages, and food must come before education.

The adult illiteracy rate is 52 percent (48 percent of males are illiterate and 52 percent of females are illiterate), so education remains a key obstacle to economic and social advancement in Haiti. Although plans for further implementation of reforms have not been abandoned, the current economic and political crises in Haiti have overshadowed educational concerns. Unless this trend is reversed, Haiti will continue to be dependent upon other benevolent nations for aid.

The Benefits of Education for Haiti

Early Haitians were correct in their assessment that education was vital to their success as a nation. When the people are kept in the dark educationally, their capacity to effectively contribute to governing their national future is severely limited. In fact, illiteracy is a form of slavery. Haitians demonstrated their resolve to be free of slavery in the revolt that culminated with the establishment of the world's first black republic. Now, the challenge before the nation is to again revolt against the slavery that is choking the very life out of the *Jewell of the Antilles*.

When literacy is on the rise, attention begins to shift from the daily struggle to survive to understanding how to prevent hunger in the future. This in turn generates creative ideas about how to tackle the challenging problems that underlie the food and fuel shortages plaguing the nation.

Today, Haiti must import 75 percent of their food. Why? The lush forests have been decimated in large part to provide charcoal for use in household cooking. This deforestation has caused severe erosion from storm runoff, which washes topsoil out to sea. With topsoil gone, farmland becomes sterile and will not produce crops. When crops are unable to grow, people who would benefit from the crop (sellers and buyers) go hungry. Thus, when people look out only for themselves and their families, little thought is given to the larger question, "What will we do when…?"

Individual consciousness grows with education to encompass other families, communities, regions and the nation as a whole. Thus, an educated populace would look at the issue of deforestation and determine that basic changes must occur in Haitian households in order to secure their future. The first logical question to be asked is whether charcoal is the best choice of cooking fuel. If so, then the next question, "How can we ensure that our supply of wood to make charcoal is regularly replenished?" will lead to action by the people.

This is just one example of how consciousness grows with education. Another example is in the area of health and cleanliness.

> *Individual consciousness grows with education to encompass other families, communities, regions and the nation as a whole.*

Understanding how impure water affects health leads communities to take action to ensure water supplies are clean and kept that way. Proper hygiene practices are implemented helping to reduce infection from other diseases, which make the community healthier. Other benefits of education include:

- Fewer incidents of addiction and substance abuse
- Reduced juvenile delinquency
- Reduced teen pregnancy
- Reductions in violent behavior and physical abuse

In short, people begin to take their individual actions more seriously with the understanding that what they do affects others. Greater consciousness of the larger good motivates people to goodwill and good works toward others. People are motivated to succeed in life as they succeed in school, thus laying a foundation for successful families, businesses, churches, communities, etc.

Haiti's New Generation

Right now there is a new generation in Haiti that is unsatisfied with the status quo. This group of young people is not willing to remain the way they are, and are willing to work hard to fulfill their dreams. These young men and women are fearless in their determination to succeed and refuse to take no for an answer. Like Martin Luther King, Jr., they have been to the mountaintop, looked over the other side and have seen the Promised Land. They know that Haiti's vast resource of human might and power has never been directed to building a strong and vibrant nation.

Repression, brutality and corruption was the legacy left by Duvalierism, but Haiti's new generation is raising a new standard. Collectively and individually, they rise up and shout, *"NO! Haiti is destined for greatness. Teach us. Mentor us. Guide us. Direct us. We will lead our great nation of Haiti into her future of abundance, prosperity and success!"*

Mighty leaders are being developed in the schools of Haiti. How many more would be if the resources were in place for them to be trained and mentored? The voices of Haiti's past shout from the pages of history, "Our young must be educated!" The voices of Haiti's youth today shout the same message, "Teach us! Mentor us! Guide us! Direct us!" The new generation is Haiti's new vision.

Leadership Treasure #6

Knowledge is one of the greatest assets of a leader—the use of knowledge is his pathway to the future. This is why true leaders never stop seeking and sharing. They understand that leadership requires constant listening, learning, and growing our minds.

Haiti teaches that embracing the truth and renewing the mind is vital to achieve our potential. Don't listen to lies.

Chapter Seven

Hope Renewed – Audacious Dreams

"For I know the plans I have for you,"
declares the LORD, "plans to prosper you and
not to harm you, plans to give you hope and a
future." (Jeremiah 29:11 NIV)

Haiti's youth are catching the vision. No longer oppressed by a dictator's irrational fear, these bright young people are beginning to rise and shine. For them, the sun has risen above the horizon and darkness no longer holds the land captive.

Are there challenges to face? Does hunger and poverty blight the land? Is the infrastructure of the nation crumbling? Yes. Yes. And yes. But in the light of a new day, these problems are not viewed as insurmountable. Vision enables these young people to see through the problems to their solution, just as Jesus *"who for the joy set before Him endured the cross,*

scorning its shame, and sat down at the right hand of the throne of God" (Heb. 12:2).

Our Response – Our Choice

Just as Haiti's youth are choosing to take up the banner of hope and press for change, we have a choice. We can look at the problems - inefficient government, corruption, hunger, poverty, sickness, disease, Voodoo paganism - and choose to be part of the solution or part of the problem.

Choosing to do nothing is a choice to be part of the problem. Knowledge coupled with inaction is tantamount to abandonment.

Choosing to be part of the solution means taking the knowledge you have gained from this book and other sources and then finding ways to assist. This may mean financial support of organizations—religious, secular, governmental—who are engaged on the ground in Haiti working to solve the nation's problems. It may mean going to Haiti to assist in redemptive projects that help change the floods of failure into rivers of success. It may mean praying and interceding for a nation that God is mindful of, so that His promises and His will may be done on earth as it is in Heaven.

The key is making a choice!

Gideon's Choice

Scripture tells the amazing story of a man named Gideon (Judges 6-8). During his life, Israel suffered under the oppression of the Midianites, a violent and blood-thirsty people. These people would take what they wanted and burn the rest, leaving Israel desolate. The Israelite children were taken to be used as sacrifices to the demon gods of Midian, the women taken as slaves, and the men killed. Livestock was either stolen by the Midianites or slaughtered and left to rot on the ground.

One day, Gideon set out to go to a hidden place where he could thresh his wheat without being seen by the enemy. On his way, Gideon met the Angel of the Lord who greeted him... *"The Lord is with you, mighty warrior"* (Judges 6:12). Gideon was a little upset with the greeting and asked a question that most of us ask the Lord on a regular basis: *"Why? If God is with us, then why are our crops burned, our children murdered, our wives taken and the men slaughtered?"*

The Angel of the Lord didn't answer "Why?" but instead told Gideon to *"Go in the strength you have and save Israel out of Midian's hand. Am I not sending you?"* (v. 14).

Though Gideon thought of himself as the weakest man in Israel, he believed what the Lord said. Gideon accepted the call of God to save Israel, so he stepped out. He moved forward. Were all his questions answered? Did everything run smoothly for him? Did all the problems just evaporate because Gideon said he would go? No. No. And no! But Gideon's faith in God's promise kept him going. Vision enabled him to see through the challenges to the solution. He endured the hardship to take hold of the promise!

We are no different than Gideon. We are sometimes weak and timid, afraid to move out and confront the challenges before us. However, God's promise to be with us is very real. As we partner with Him where He is already at work, mercy and grace for the task at hand is in abundance (Matt. 28:18-20; Mark 16:15-20).

> *A banner hanging nearby read, "Haiti: Hope in God."*

Answering the Call

One couple who answered the call did so during the waning days of Jean-Claude Duvalier.

It all started with five tents pitched under a grove of coconut trees. A banner hanging nearby read, *"Haiti: Hope in God."* The year was 1983 and the tents belonged to George and Jeanne DeTellis, who had left the United States after 25 years in the pastorate to pioneer New Missions in Haiti. Who could have imagined how God would bless such humble beginnings!

Today, those five tents are a distant memory. Over 50 buildings later, New Missions has 21 churches, a medical clinic, 21 preschools, 21 elementary schools, a high school, a Bible college, business school, and a Missions Training Center for hosting visiting teams.

Over 9,000 students are enrolled in New Missions schools. Approximately 1,000 people are cared for each month through the medical clinic ministry. New

Missions employs over 300 Haitians to teach, preach, and meet the needs of their own people.

New Missions is being used by God to help raise up a new generation that will literally change the course of Haiti's history... and eternity.

Imagine what God can do with your willing heart. He is already at work in the lives of a new generation of Haitian youth, fearless in their pursuit of a "future and a hope" as promised by God in Jeremiah 29:11.

The Stakes Are High

"What is at stake?" The future of a nation hinged on a generation of young people who are destined to become the leaders of Haiti.

Now it is time for you to answer the call. How will you use the information you have gleaned from this book? This is about far more than Haiti; it is about your response to God in the world around you. Will you press into the fray and use your God-given talents, abilities, wealth and resources for His cause? Or will you, like the armed men of Ephraim (Psalm 78:9) turn back on the day of battle?

"What is at stake?" you may ask. The future of a nation hinged on a generation of young people who are destined to become the leaders of Haiti. You, by partnering with God in this great cause, have the opportunity to be a history maker...a nation shaper. Leaders are emerging and more are to come. You can make a difference in helping them choose whom to follow. Will it be God?

Real leadership starts with service and you can be a leader that makes a difference right where you are. When opportunity comes your way, will you respond with how can I take or how can I serve? As this book reflects on Haiti's history, we learn from both success and failures. Be a life-long learner, reaching toward what is in front of you with great passion and dedication to serve those under your care.

Leadership Treasure #7

Leaders must continually be under development. When a leader thinks he has "arrived" failure is imminent.

Haiti teaches that positive change requires taking a risk and being a bold leader of great faith.

Epilogue

When we study the history of Haiti we see how corruption, greed and pride led to the stripping of a lush garden, the *Pearl of the Antilles*, and turned it into a wasteland. Haiti contributed more to the wealth of Europe than all of the 13 colonies combined. Now it is the poorest nation in the Western Hemisphere.

The people who pay the highest price for the luxury of their leaders are those at the bottom of the social ladder—the poorest of the poor. Corrupt, prideful leaders turned away from the poor and used the wealth of the nation to enrich themselves and their closest associates - leaving nothing behind to build infrastructure, create jobs, or nourish the masses. This drain on the economy of Haiti is like a voracious cancer that consumes all that is healthy and good around it.

Today, Haiti is at a crossroad. How will the people respond? How will the world respond? How will you respond?

I invite you to invest in the future of Haiti. This can be done several ways, but one that is very close to my heart is the "Yes Haiti" project. This program provides scholarships to high school students at this critical stage in their lives to assist in their spiritual, social, and community development. We are training new leaders.

You will help empower them through your gift. For more information on the "Yes Haiti" project, call 1-800-Yes-Haiti or visit www.yeshaiti.com.

Has the leader inside of you been energized? Your success and the success of Haiti is very close to my heart. Godly leadership is paramount in the development of godly families, communities and nations. The primary lesson learned from Haiti is the choice that each leader must make. The pearl of leadership is servanthood; the poison of leadership is pride. Today, lead with the heart of a servant that looks to help others fulfill their dream.

Tim DeTellis is available for speaking engagements and personal appearances. To contact Tim or to feature him as the keynote speaker of your next event, contact:

Gloria Leyda
Ambassador Speakers Bureau & Literary Agency
PHONE: 615-370-4700 x235
EMAIL: gloria@ambassadorspeakers.com

For more information you may also visit Tim's website:
www.timdetellis.com

To purchase additional copies of this book or other books published by Advantage Books call our toll free order number at:
1-888-383-3110 (Book Orders Only)

or visit our bookstore website at:
www.advbookstore.com

Longwood, Florida, USA
"we bring dreams to life"™
www.advbooks.com